© Scripture Union 2021
ISBN 978 1 78506 838 6

Scripture Union England and Wales
Trinity House, Opal Court, Opal Drive, Fox Milne,
Milton Keynes, MK15 0DF
email: info@scriptureunion.org.uk
www.scriptureunion.org.uk

British Library Cataloguing-in-Publication Data
A catalogue record of this book is available from the British Library.

Unless otherwise marked, Scripture quotations are taken from the Contemporary English Version published by HarperCollins Publishers © 1991, 1992, 1995 American Bible Society

Scripture quotations marked ICB are taken from The Holy Bible, International Children's Bible Copyright © 1986, 1988, 1999, 2015 by Tommy Nelson, a division of Thomas Nelson. Used by permission.

Printed and bound by Melita Press, Malta
Cover and internal design: heatherknight.me.uk

Pictures credits:
Cover: photo - wavebreakmedia/Shutterstock, decorative border - whatzapa/Shutterstock
Photos: p13 - Coscaron/Istockphoto, p21 - Anastasiya Aleksandrenko/Shutterstock, p25 - Choreograph/Istockphoto, p49 juggling balls - Westlight/Istockphoto, p22, p29, p46, p56 - Pexels. All other photos Unsplash.
Graphics: owls - seasoning–17/Shutterstock, scribble circles and arrows - Freepik, pickaxe - Dmytro Vyshnevskyi/Istockphoto, spade - Macrovector/Istockphoto, map marker - Devita ayu Silvianingtyan/Istockphoto, lightbulb - mactrunk/Istockphoto, emojis - kaleo/Shutterstock , note page and notebook - Insh1na/Istockphoto

With special thanks to contributors Sarah Davison and Leanne Sheppard.

Scripture Union is an international Christian charity working with churches in more than 130 countries.

Thank you for purchasing this book. Any profits from this book support SU in England and Wales to bring the good news of Jesus Christ to children, young people and families and to enable them to meet God through the Bible and prayer. Find out more about our work and how you can get involved at:
www.scriptureunion.org.uk (England and Wales)
www.suscotland.org.uk (Scotland)
www.suni.co.uk (Northern Ireland)
www.scriptureunion.org (USA)
www.su.org.au (Australia)

Leaders' Guide

Rooted Junior

Rooted Junior is not a programme. It is not something that you 'do' for ten weeks with a group of children.

Rooted Junior is a way of being, a way of thinking about long-term relational ministry with children, particularly those aged 8 to 11. Rooted Junior works in any context, with any level of faith development and with any level of ability.

Rooted Junior is adaptable, accessible, invitational and creative.

The Rooted Junior material places the child at the centre. It seeks to provide space for that child to grow, flourish and be nurtured in a safe, committed and compassionate Christian community.

Rooted Junior aims to unlock potential in each child, enabling them to be the very best version of themselves, helping them to become all that God intended them to be.

Rooted Junior invites children to explore who they are and why they matter, while making space for them to wrestle with the big questions of life.

As a Rooted Junior leader, you have the privilege of journeying alongside these children and helping them in their exploration, while sharing something of your own journey so far.

You will notice that there is very little in the way of explicit 'faith discussion' or 'God-slot'-type material included in this resource. Instead, within the material for each session you will find several questions listed as part of the 'DIG DEEPER' section. These questions can be used *during* the other activities in your session, helping you to naturally, authentically and appropriately share your own experiences of how faith and life meld together.

Rooted Junior isn't about the activities you 'do', the venue you 'inhabit' or indeed the resources you can provide. It is about journeying with the children in your group, giving space and opportunity for genuine conversations and meaningful long-term relationships.

The Rooted Junior material in this resource covers ten key themes (outlined on the following page) and is designed in a way that is adaptable to any context in which you are working. The suggestions for activities are exactly that – suggestions, so you should expect to mould and shape them to suit your context and the children you are working with. Several alternative activities are included within each session, if you need a few extra ideas! The last session will help you to encourage the children to dream big, reflect on their lives so far and inspire them for the next adventure that awaits!

If you're not already in contact with a group of children, check out our collection of resources at www.su.org.uk for ideas and advice on running your own Rooted Junior Hub. A Rooted Junior Hub is a tried and tested way of helping you make initial connections with 8- to 11-year-olds in your area.

I pray that God will use you to share his love with children as they discover the difference Jesus can make to the challenges and adventures in life.

Lucy Pearson

Scripture Union, Greater Manchester Mission Enabler
Rooted and Rooted Junior Pioneer

CONTENTS

WHERE DO I BEGIN?

A few questions to consider before embarking on the Rooted Junior journey...

- Who are you working with? Why are you doing this? (Check out our collection of resources at www.su.org.uk for ideas and advice, and read the section on initial connections and running your own Rooted Junior Hub at the back of this book.)

- Who will work with you on your Rooted Junior team?

- Where will you meet?

- What resources do you have?

- What are the children expecting?

- How will you explain to the children what Rooted Junior is?

- Are these children exploring faith?

- Are there any issues that you want to focus on?

- How might you adapt some of the material in this resource to better suit your context? (Eg if the group you are working with doesn't enjoy creativity, what types of activity would they enjoy? Perhaps sport, drama, outdoor activities etc. How can you make sure your activities will help you to relay the message?)

- Have you made sure that your group gatherings will adhere to the safeguarding policies of your organisation? What additional pastoral support will you offer? (You might consider a mentoring programme and/or referrals to other agencies or key workers.)

- What's next?

Using the *Rooted Junior Leaders' Guide*

The sessions are designed to be easily adapted for your context. Feel free to change the activities, swap sessions around or adapt the order. The key thing is that you create space for the children to unpack some of the themes and thoughts in their own time and in an environment that is comfortable for them. Having said that, do remember that developing a bit of a routine for each session will help the children to feel safe and at ease.

As the children arrive at your meeting venue, it can be helpful to have a selection of activities available for them to engage with straight away (such as colouring, printed quizzes, simple board games etc), particularly if the children in the group don't know each other very well. If you are able to do this every time you meet it may help the children know what to expect, reducing any potential anxiety or nervousness.

As your group progresses through the Rooted Junior sessions outlined in this guide, they will hopefully feel more confident in sharing their thoughts and feelings with one another. But this isn't always easy, and you should consider the use of some other tools that allow children to explain how they are feeling without having to say too much. For example, you could incorporate an emoji wall into your meeting space and encourage children to use it both at the beginning and throughout your time together.

1 Create an emoji wall for your group by printing out various emojis and sticking them on to a large sheet of paper to create a chart.

2 Print or write the first name of each child in your group on a slip of paper. Affix a small piece of sticky tack to each name.

3 Stick your emoji chart on the wall of your meeting space, and attach the name slips to one corner of your chart using the sticky tack.

4 As the children arrive (and throughout your time together) encourage them to place their name next to an emoji that represents how they are feeling.

5 Invite the children to talk with you about their emoji choice, if they would like to. (If they would prefer not to talk about their choice, that's also fine!)

Within each session outline you will find the following sections:

OBJECTIVES

what you might achieve by using this session.

ICEBREAKER

a game or activity that gets everyone involved and helps them get to know one another.

THEME

an opportunity to unpack the theme and explore it as a whole group.

REFLECTION

time to get creative, expressive or active, while chatting through what has been explored. (Doing something practical while talking with those around you makes natural conversation easier.)

DIG DEEPER

optional questions to help children consider their own faith journey.

FURTHER IDEAS

suggestions for alternative activities based on the theme of the session. (You may find that certain themes really resonate with the children in your context. Don't rush past these – allow time for your group to explore them more deeply. The ideas in this section may be especially useful in this scenario.)

Some of the themes unpacked in Rooted Junior may be challenging for certain children, so be prepared for some difficult but honest conversations. Make sure there is some support in place for children who may need it (in line with your organisation's safeguarding policy). This may include external agencies, mentoring programmes or further groups that are specifically tailored towards children's needs.

SESSION 1

What's my name?

OBJECTIVES

For the group to get to know one another and gain an understanding of what their time together will be about.

For the leaders to gain an understanding of the group dynamic.

ICEBREAKER

Begin your session with one of the following activities or games:

We will rock you!

1 Invite the children to sit in a circle.

2 As the leader, start the game by tapping your legs twice with your hands, then clapping once. When you clap, say your name.

3 Tap your legs twice again, then clap once, but this time say the name of someone else in the group.

4 Encourage the person you named to tap their legs twice and say their name, then tap their legs twice again, clap, and say the name of someone else in the group.

5 The game continues until everyone has been 'named'.

> **TIP**
> This game is a good way of learning names and encouraging your group to concentrate!

Object game

You will need: several random objects that can be easily picked up in one hand

1 Place the objects in the middle of the room.

2 Give each item a number value (but don't reveal the scoring system to the to the rest of the group).

3 Split the group into teams of six (adding leaders to make up team numbers if needed).

4 Number each team member sequentially from one to six.

TIP
After a few rounds you may find that team members all start trying to pick up the same object – guessing that it is worth the most. If this happens, don't miss the opportunity to start a discussion on what 'worth' really is.

5 When you call their number, invite the team member to run to the pile of objects, choose one object, pick it up with one hand and return with the object to their team.

6 After all objects have been collected, announce the total score for each team (using your secret scoring system).

7 Play several rounds or until you feel the children have had enough. The children should begin to learn which objects are more 'valuable' than others.

What's in a name?

You will need: a printed list of the first names of the children in the group and their meanings

1 Ask one person to say their name.

2 Invite the rest of the group to guess what the name means.

3 If no one guesses correctly, share the meaning of the name from your list.

4 Continue until everyone's name has been discussed.

TIP
This can lead to discussion on whether the children think their name describes their character.

THEME

My name

You will need: pens, pencils, art materials, paper, a list of the meaning of all the names of the children in your group

Invite the children to write their name on a sheet of paper in bubble writing. Suggest they decorate it using the art materials provided. As they write and decorate, discuss the following questions together:

- What does your name mean? (Use your list if necessary.)
- Do you know how or why your name was chosen?
- If you could have chosen your name, what would it be?
- Do you think God knows your name?

REFLECTION

My mood board

You will need: pens, pencils, art materials, safety scissors, glue sticks, paper, old magazines or catalogues

TIP
Why not place several *Rooted Junior Hub Cards* around your meeting space to encourage discussion while the group are creating?

Explain that a mood board is a collage of images, colours and text that is themed around a specific idea or person.

Invite the children to create their own mood boards, representing their interests, using the materials provided.

DIG DEEPER

Select the faith-based questions from the *Rooted Junior Hub Cards* and discuss them with the children. Make a note of the cards you choose for this activity and the answers given as you will be revisiting these in Session 10.

FURTHER IDEAS

My name mug
Invite each child to decorate a mug with their name.

Name bingo
Create your own bingo cards using the names in your group, and play bingo with them during the whole session.

ROOTED JUNIOR JOURNAL

If you are using the *Rooted Junior Journal* with your group, you could include some time in your session for the children to work through pages 7 to 12. Alternatively, you could encourage the children to work through these pages at home, between sessions, if they would like to.

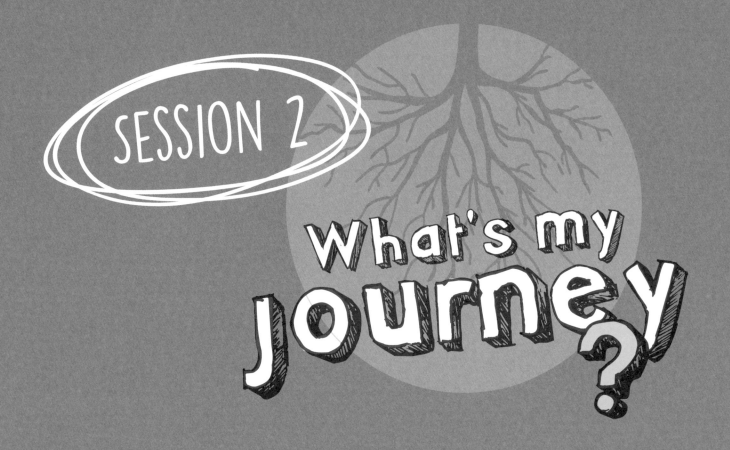

SESSION 2

What's my Journey?

OBJECTIVES

For children to understand that their personal journey matters, and that the small things are as important as the big things in life.

ICEBREAKER

Begin your session with one of the following activities or games:

Crocodile swamp

You will need: a chair, an item of clothing, a blanket or sheet, a large sheet of card/paper

1 Set up an obstacle course that goes from one side of your meeting space to the other using different types of objects as obstacles. (Ensure the objects are items that can easily be stood on or carried.)

2 Ask the group to stand on one side of the room and tell them they need to imagine the floor is a crocodile swamp or hot lava.

3 Explain that the aim is to find a path to the other side of the room, using the objects on the floor as stepping stones, without falling into the crocodile swamp or lava.

4 Say that if anyone falls in, the whole group must start again.

5 Time the first crossing attempt and, if successful, challenge the group to beat their previous time on their second attempt.

You could play this game as one team working together or in multiple teams racing against each other.

Stepping stones

You will need: double sheets of newspaper or pillowcases

1 Divide the group into small teams of around four to six people.

2 Ask the teams to line up along one side of the room.

TIP
Try not to give the game away unless the group are really struggling. Obviously, the solution involves teamwork, sending some of the team across, then going back for the others.

3   Give each group two fewer newspaper sheets or pillowcases than the number of people in the team (eg for a team of six, provide four sheets of newspaper or pillowcases).

4   Explain to the children that the newspaper sheets or pillowcases are 'stones', which must be used to help each team cross from one side of the room to the other. Any member of the team can hold as many stones as they wish. Only one person can stand on a stone at a time.

5   Tell the teams that they need to work out as a group how they will get from one side of the room to the other with only one person on a stone at a time.

6   The first team to successfully transport every member from one side of the room to the other, without breaking any of the rules, wins the game.

'Follow-me' tag

1   Ask the children to spread out and sit on the floor away from each other.

2   Explain that you will pick someone to be the 'runner' and someone to be the 'catcher', and that the object of the game is for the runner to run away from the catcher and avoid being caught.

TIP
You could play this game using a timer – giving each catcher only 2 minutes to catch the runner before swapping with someone else.

3 Say that the other players are spaced out around the floor as obstacles to run around.

4 Tell the children that the catcher MUST follow exactly the same path as the runner and cannot catch them unless they have done this – even if the runner runs past them! Other players can give directions to the catcher and must shout if the catcher goes wrong.

5 Play as many rounds as time allows or until the children lose enthusiasm for the game.

THEME

A changing journey

You will need: pens, pencils, art materials, pictures of: acorns, oak trees, caterpillars, butterflies

Place the pictures in front of the children and challenge them to point out the changes that have taken place. (The acorn turning into the oak tree and the caterpillar turning into the butterfly.)

Explain that you will spend some time thinking about the changes that have happened in the children's lives as they have grown older.

Draw a timeline on a sheet of paper that represents your own life – adding significant events along the line.

Show the children your timeline and explain that you would like them to create a similar diagram that represents their life so far. If the children are unsure what to include, you could suggest things like starting school, the birth

of siblings, holidays, special trips, injuries, sports events or achievements, joining clubs etc.

For younger children, you might like to suggest they draw rather than write on their timeline.

As the children create their timelines discuss the following questions together:

- How have you changed in the last year (physical changes, teachers, friends, interests and activities etc)?
- What impact have these changes had on you?
- Does change feel like a good thing or a bad thing? Why?

TIP
Be aware that some children's life journey won't follow the same pattern as others, but remind them that this makes us all unique.

REFLECTION

You will need: disposable cups or small plant pots, seeds such as cress (or something similar), compost or cotton wool, water

Give each child a cup or plant pot and a few seeds.

Explain that they are going to plant the seeds (using compost or cotton wool) and then take them home, care for them and watch them grow.

Place the compost or cotton wool and water in a central place that the children can reach easily.

As the children plant their seeds, discuss the following questions together:

- What will help the seeds to grow (food, light, being kept in the right location etc)?

- What do you think helps people to grow – not just in height, but in their personality and wellbeing too (food, love, safety, education etc)?

DIG DEEPER

As the group plant their seeds, read Matthew 6:25,26. Then discuss the following questions together:

- Do you think God has anything to do with your life?

- If you were to thank God for something or someone, what or who would it be?

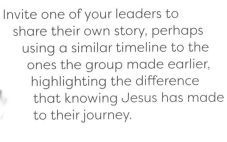

- If you could ask God one thing, what would it be?

Invite one of your leaders to share their own story, perhaps using a similar timeline to the ones the group made earlier, highlighting the difference that knowing Jesus has made to their journey.

Bird feeder
Invite the children to make a bird feeder using recycled materials (you could watch this video for ideas: https://www.youtube.com/watch?v=F5KQCJGEYeA).

ROOTED JUNIOR JOURNAL

If you are using the *Rooted Junior Journal* with your group, you could include some time in your session for the children to work through pages 13 to 16. Alternatively, you could encourage the children to work through these pages at home, between sessions, if they would like to.

TIP
As a group, explore the possibility of going on a trip. Think about the types of things to include in the planning, and assign each child or small group a different responsibility to research, eg transport, food, costs, timings.

SESSION 3

What do I feel?

OBJECTIVES

For the children to have a safe space to explore their emotions and look at coping strategies and techniques.

ICEBREAKER

Begin your session with one of the following activities or games:

Reactions

You will need: a space large enough for the children to spread out and a set of emoji images or cards

1 Place the emoji images or cards around the walls of your meeting space.

2 Read out one of the scenarios below and ask the children to decide how they would react in that situation.

3 Invite the children to run to the emoji that best represents their response.

4 If you run out of scenarios and the children are keen to keep playing, make up your own!

- Being given a massive ice cream covered in lots of chocolates and sweets and sauce!

- Having to watch Peppa Pig with your little sister over and over again.

- Going on a big roller-coaster and sitting in the front row.

- Being told off for something you didn't do.

- One of your favourite toys getting broken.

- A power cut that means all internet and electrics stop working in your house (and it lasts for 3 hours!).

Arches game

1 Split the group into pairs and ask each pair to stand facing each other with their arms raised and hands touching – forming an arch large enough for other children to run through.

2 Ask all the pairs to arrange themselves in a row, so that a series of arches is formed.

3 Allocate a number to each pair, and explain that the children on one side of the arch are team A and the children on the opposite side are team B.

4 Say that when you call out a number, the pair with that number should break their arch, run up the inside of the archway (towards the pair with the highest number) and then run around the back of those forming the archway, back to their 'spot'. The first person from the pair to stand with the arms raised wins a point for their team.

5 The game ends when all pairs have had a turn.

TIP
Instead of numbering the pairs you could give each pair a particular emotion as their name. Then tell a short, made-up story that randomly includes some of those names. When the pair hear their emotion they should proceed to run through the archway and back to their 'spot', as described above.

Emotions

You will need: coloured pens, pencils, a large sheet of paper

This activity invites children to think about how different emotions feel in their body.

Ask for a volunteer and invite the children to draw around that person on a large sheet of paper.

Encourage the children to write lots of different emotions around the person outline they have created.

Ask the children to choose the colour pen that they feel matches each emotion, and invite them to draw lines to link the different emotions to the part of the body where they think that might be felt (eg feeling angry might be felt in the hands, if they are clenched).

REFLECTION

You will need: pens, pencils, paper, tissue paper, glue sticks, stickers, sticker jewels, felt-tip pens, scissors, empty glass jars

Talk to the group about how it's easy for our emotions to feel like they are taking over and, when this happens, we might react in ways that aren't always helpful and don't make us feel better.

Explain that you are going to spend some time making 'jars of joy' together.

Give each child an empty glass jar and encourage them to decorate it using the materials available.

Hand out small slips of paper and invite the children to write one thing on each slip that helps them to feel positive (eg going for a walk, playing outside, reading a book, baking, watching Netflix). After writing on a slip, encourage the children to fold it up and place it in their jar. If appropriate for your group, you might like to provide some pre-printed Bible verses on slips of paper for them to include in their jars.

Explain to the children that their jars of joy are there to help in times when emotions feel overwhelming. You might like to use the following words:

If you're ever feeling like your emotions are taking over, find your jar of joy and pick out a slip of paper. Do what it says and notice how it changes the way you feel. Some time later, when your emotions have changed for the better, notice what you've learned about yourself.

TIP
Be aware that, for some children, talking about how they cope with difficult emotions may be challenging. If you feel this activity may be unhelpful for your group, replace it with one of the further ideas from pages 22 and 23.

DIG DEEPER

As the group create their jars of joy, discuss the following questions together, either individually or in small groups.

- Have you ever spoken to God?

- Would you ever share how you feel with God? Why, or why not?

- Do you think God experiences emotions?

Invite one of your leaders to share their own story, including a time when they struggled to cope with their emotions, highlighting the difference that knowing Jesus has made. You could suggest they include the story of a Bible character who struggled with difficult emotions. (Eg Moses got angry, and even though he was right to be angry as there was something bad happening, his actions were not always the right way of expressing that emotion.)

FURTHER IDEAS

Worry sorting

1 Ask the children to write their top five worries on individual slips of paper. Then encourage them to sort their slips into three piles, as follows:

- worries that are someone else's responsibility, eg a teacher, an adult

- worries that are for later, eg such as a school move or getting a job when they're older

- worries they can do something about now, eg homework, friendship issues.

2 Work with the children to plan practical things they can do to address the worries they can do something about now, while also talking together about the other worries.

Drama scenes

Explain to the children that you are going to play a game in which they create the scenes you describe in groups consisting of a certain number.

Read out the following scenes, specifying a group size and the time allowed at random:

- In groups of ____ create the shape of people riding on a roller-coaster at a theme park. You have ____ minutes!

- In groups of ____ create the shape of people getting on a plane to go on holiday. You have ____ minutes!

- In groups of ____ create the shape of people performing in a dance troupe at school. You have ____ minutes!

Create your own additional scenes to extend the game.

When the groups have created their scene, use this an opportunity to discuss how different places and events provoke different feelings. Notice that not everyone feels the same way about each situation.

Outsider tag

1 Invite the group to stand in a circle facing inwards, with their hands behind their backs.

2 Nominate someone to walk around the circle, in a clockwise direction, and choose a 'runner' by tapping their hands.

3 Challenge the runner to then run anticlockwise around the circle, while the chooser runs in a clockwise direction (while avoiding bumping into one another!), both attempting to get back to their original space as quickly as possible.

4 The first person to get back to their original space stays there and the other person becomes the 'chooser'.

After a few rounds, encourage the children to discuss what it feels like to be an outsider, or someone who is left out of things.

ROOTED JUNIOR JOURNAL

If you are using the **Rooted Junior Journal** with your group, you could include some time in your session for the children to work through pages 17 to 22. Alternatively, you could encourage the children to work through these pages at home, between sessions, if they would like to.

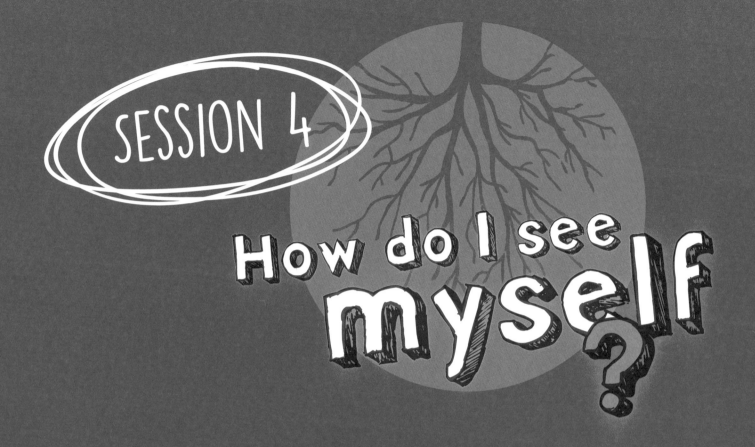

SESSION 4

How do I see myself?

OBJECTIVES

For the children to spend time recognising their strengths, and to support them as they explore their self-worth.

ICEBREAKER

Begin your session with one of the following activities or games:

Superheroes

1 Explain that they are going to play a version of 'Rock, paper, scissors', but using superheroes.

2 Challenge the group to agree actions for Batman, Spiderman and Green Lantern (or three superheroes of their choice).

3 Ask the children to form pairs, and say that Spiderman beats Batman; Batman beats Green Lantern; Green Lantern beats Spiderman (or the superheroes they have chosen).

4 On 'Go', invite each child to make an action of their choice and identify the winner for each pair.

5 Either continue playing in the original pairs, or make new pairs from the winners until you have one overall winner.

Superpower aerobics

1 Invite the children to spread out in your meeting area, so that they each have space.

2 Explain that they are going to have a superpower aerobics session.

3 Call out a series of superpower movements, such as lightning speed run on spot, power jumping jacks, invisibility floor crawls.

4 Continue for your allocated time, or until the children have had enough.

THEME

Superpowers

Ask the children what superpower they would choose, if they could have anything they wanted, and why. Challenge them to choose and demonstrate an action for their superpower.

Foil faces

You will need: aluminium foil, a stapler, staples, cardboard

Give each member of the group a piece of foil and invite them to get into pairs. Explain that they are going to help each other to make imprints of their faces in the foil.

Show them how to place the foil around their face and slowly begin to press in – doing mouth and nose last. As they gently push into the foil it will mould around their faces, leaving the shape of their face in the foil.

Afterwards, they should have a model of their face.

Talk about how people see themselves; you might like to use the following words:

Sometimes we want to change things about ourselves that we do not like *(start adapting your foil face).* **And, sometimes, there's just too much that doesn't feel right and we don't want to look at it at all** *(squash up the face).*

TIP
Make it very clear that they should not keep the foil over their faces for too long, and supervise this activity carefully.

Discuss the following questions together:

- What do you think other people think when they look at you?
- How important is it to say nice things to other people?
- What do you think God thinks when he looks at you?

To finish this activity, give each member of your group a sheet of card and help them to staple their face mould to it to take home, if they choose.

REFLECTION

Modelling clay

You will need: play dough, a timer

Give out a small ball of play dough to each child. Explain that they have just 3 minutes to create something as beautiful as possible that fits on the palm of their hand.

After 3 minutes, ask the children to imagine how they would feel if you were to walk by and squash what they have made.
Then as a whole group discuss the following questions together:

- How do you think you would feel if someone squashed your creation?
- How do you think you would feel if you squashed someone else's creation?
- It's easy to make people feel 'squashed' by the things we say to them or the way in which we treat them. What can you do to make sure the people you talk to never feel squashed?

Explain that how we value ourselves and others is really important; you might like to use the following words:

If we believe that we are not worth anything and can be easily squashed, we are missing out on our purpose in life and all that we can be and do. However, we have a choice about how we treat others with the things we say and do towards them. It's always better to build others up rather than squash them down.

Ask a leader to share a personal example of how someone treated them and how it made them feel. Challenge the children to think about how they would like to make others feel.

DIG DEEPER

As the group make their models, read Ephesians 2:10 (NLT). Then discuss the following questions together:

- What do you think it means to be God's masterpiece?
- How does that make you feel?

Ask a leader to tell the group about a time when they struggled with what others thought of them, and how God helped them to realise how he sees them.

FURTHER IDEAS

Cards

Invite the children to make an encouragement card for someone else. Suggest they write out the person's name, one letter at a time, then add something positive about them beginning with each letter (or as many as they can think of!).

Balloon burst

Give each group member a piece of string and a balloon. Invite them to blow up their balloon, attach it to the string and the string to their ankle.

Explain that the aim of the game is to keep their own balloon 'alive' while trying to burst other people's balloons.

Say that anyone whose balloon is burst must leave the playing area without bursting any more balloons.

At the end of the game, explain that this shows that how we treat others is important. Say that it's OK to want to win, but not OK to cheat (burst balloons once your balloon has burst) to do it.

ROOTED JUNIOR JOURNAL

If you are using the *Rooted Junior Journal* with your group, you could include some time in your session for the children to work through pages 23 to 28. Alternatively, you could encourage the children to work through these pages at home, between sessions, if they would like to.

Who's around me ?

OBJECTIVES

For the children to think about their friendships, and how they can be a good friend to others.

ICEBREAKER

Begin your session with one of the following activities or games:

Human knot

1 Invite everyone to stand in a circle facing inwards.

2 First ask the group to put out their right hand and join hands with another hand in the circle. Then ask them to put out their left hand and join with another hand. (This works best if they don't hold either hand of the person next to them.)

3 Encourage the group to try and untangle themselves.

Join-up tag

1 Ask the group to spread out around the room, then choose one of them to be the catcher.

2 Invite the catcher to catch another child, join hands and make a line of two.

3 Encourage the children to keep going until everyone in the room has been caught and they are all joined together in a long line. During the game, as the line gets longer, encourage them to work together and not pull each other over!

TIP
For variations, challenge the children to untangle without talking, or give them a time limit.

31

THEME

Choosing friends

You will need: printed pictures

Show the children a selection of pictures of fictional characters from books and films, such as Disney princesses, Harry Potter, Peter Pan, Tom Gates, Willy Wonka, and some pop stars, sports personalities and YouTube stars.

Ask the children to choose who of these they would be friends with. Challenge them to tell you what it is about that person that they think would make them be a good friend.

Different pictures

You will need: pens, pencils, paper

Give everyone a sheet of paper and a selection of pens. With your sheet of paper hidden from the group, draw a picture and then describe it.

Invite the children to draw what you have drawn, based on your explanation.

Share your pictures and encourage the group to discuss why everyone's picture has some differences.

TIP
To build some friendly competition, you could set a time limit of 30 seconds for the children to complete their picture.

Discuss the following questions together:

- Why do people hear the same words but think it means something different?

- Is it important to understand what your friends really mean when they say something?

What makes a good friend?

You will need: pens, pencils, paper

Ask the children to think of words that come to mind when describing a good friend – you could give them a few to start them off, such as 'kind', 'helpful' and 'reliable'. Encourage them to draw around their own hand on a sheet of paper, and write a word on each finger and thumb that describes a quality they would like a best friend to have. Then challenge them to think about how they can be a good friend to those around them.

Friendship blocks

You will need: pens, paper, sticky tape, building block game

Write words that are characteristics of a good friend on the blocks from a tower building game.

TIP
If you don't want to spoil your blocks, you could use pencil, or tape the words on to the blocks.

While the group are playing the game, ask them what happens when we take away the good parts of a friendship.

Card to a friend

You will need: thin card, pens, paper, tissue paper, glue sticks, stickers, sticker jewels, felt-tip pens, scissors

Using the craft materials, invite the group to create a card to give to a friend with everything they are thankful for about that friendship. While they are making the cards, ask them about friendships, the highs and the lows, the good friendships and the ones they are struggling with.

As the group make their cards, discuss the following questions together:

- Do you think God could be a friend?

- Have you ever talked to God? Do you think he listened?

- What sort of thing would you like to tell God about?

Ask one of the leaders to share a story about how God is a friend to them, perhaps with a personal testimony or by sharing a story from the Bible. They could also explain how they talk to God, and that this is what Christians call 'prayer'.

Friendship bracelets/bands
Encourage the children to make a friendship bracelet for a friend out of coloured thread. (Instructions for various styles are available online.)

Obstacle course
Set up an inside relay obstacle course, for teams of two, with one player blindfolded and the other giving instructions to navigate the course.

Teams
Encourage a discussion on how the dynamic of a sports team can affect the outcome of a game.

Concertina people
Show the children how to make a line of concertina people. Invite them to decorate their people, writing on each one a word to describe what makes a good friend.

ROOTED JUNIOR JOURNAL

If you are using the **Rooted Junior Journal** with your group, you could include some time in your session for the children to work through pages 29 to 34. Alternatively, you could encourage the children to work through these pages at home, between sessions, if they would like to.

SESSION 6

What's around me ?

OBJECTIVES

For the children to explore and reflect on what influences them in their everyday life.

ICEBREAKER

Begin your session with one of the following activities or games:

Dodgeball run-through

You will need: cones or marker tape, a selection of soft balls

1 Create a playing area using cones or marker tape – you will need to mark the ends and the sides of your chosen area.

2 Divide the children into two groups, and explain that the aim is for players in one group to run from one end of the hall to the other, while being targeted by the other players on the sidelines throwing balls. Players may only get hit (waist down!) in the set playing area.

3 Invite any player who gets hit to join the throwers at the side, until only one runner is left.

4 Make sure everyone gets a turn at both running and throwing.

Bodyguard dodgeball

You will need: a selection of soft balls

1 Ask the group to stand in a circle facing one another, and choose someone to be president/queen/equivalent!

2 Invite the chosen player to pick one or two people to be their bodyguards.

3 Challenge those left in the circle to throw balls around between themselves with the aim of trying to hit the president. Encourage the bodyguards to do all they can to defend their president.

4 When the president has been hit, choose a new president and play the game again.

TIP
You could teach the group some easy breathing techniques to help them to keep calm when they are feeling anxious. (A quick search online will give you plenty of options.)

Discussion

When you have played a couple of games, bring your group together and discuss the following questions:

- In these games you had to dodge balls at certain points to avoid getting hit. How did you cope when things came towards you? What tactics did you put into place?

- When you think about your daily life, how do you cope and react when things aren't going the way you planned?

- How can you adapt or protect yourself from things that happen unexpectedly?

Self-portrait

You will need: paper, pencils and coloured pens

Explain that in this session they are going to be thinking about how things around us can influence us, often without realising.

Give everyone a sheet of paper and invite them to draw a quick self-portrait, leaving space around their picture to write.

Challenge them to think about what other things or people influence them day by day, and encourage them draw or write

these things around their self-portrait. If they need ideas, suggest things like family, things they watch, read, activities they do, games they play, teams they belong to, school.

As the children draw their pictures, discuss the following questions together:

- Are these things all good influences?
- What makes something or someone a good or bad influence?
- How can you say yes to good things and no to people leading you to bad choices?
- How does saying yes or no make you feel?

REFLECTION

You will need: paper, pencils and coloured pens

Ask the children to continue looking at their self-portrait and the things written or drawn around it.

With a selection of different coloured pens to represent their feelings, invite the children to draw circles around each of the things showing the way they make them feel. They could, for example, use yellow to represent being happy, red for angry or sad. Encourage them to choose their own colours, and include things like jealous, spiteful and kind.

Reflect back on the icebreaker games and explore the role of the bodyguards and how they protected the president/queen from being hit. You might like to use the following words:

When we think about how things around us can influence us, it's

important for us to think about how we can guard our hearts and minds from things that are unhelpful. All the different things we interact with in our life day by day have an impact on us – on how we feel and how we behave. So, it's important for us to think about how we control what comes at us – how we can defend ourselves from things that are unhelpful (like using bodyguards!) and how we can focus on the good things that are helpful and encouraging to us.

DIG DEEPER

As the group work on the things around their self-portrait, read Ephesians 6:10–18. Then invite them to pick one or two of the things they have circled and share why they have chosen those particular things.

Ask one of the leaders to give an example of how the Bible passage has helped them in their lives.

FURTHER IDEAS

ROOTED JUNIOR JOURNAL

If you are using the *Rooted Junior Journal* with your group, you could include some time in your session for the children to work through pages 36 to 40. Alternatively, you could encourage the children to work through these pages at home, between sessions, if they would like to.

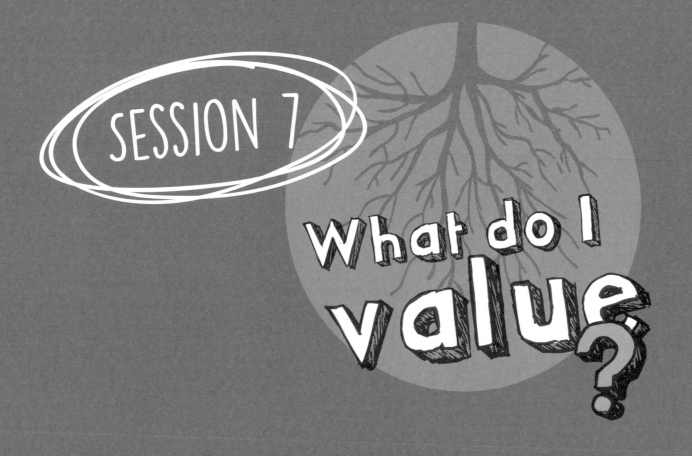

SESSION 7

What do I value?

OBJECTIVES

For the children to celebrate who they are and how they have been made, physically, mentally and spiritually.

ICEBREAKER

Begin your session with one of the following activities or games:

Fruit salad

You will need: chairs

1 Make a circle of chairs, one per child, facing inwards, and invite the children to sit down.

2 Consecutively name each of the children 'apple', 'orange' or 'pear'.

3 Call out the name of one of these fruit and challenge everyone who is that fruit to get up quickly and change places.

4 Continue calling out one of the three fruit, but occasionally call 'fruit salad', inviting everyone to stand up and swap places quickly.

A few of my favourite things

You will need: pictures of sweet foods and ingredients

1 Place your pictures of different foods and ingredients around the room (eg sweets, ice cream, fruit, chocolate).

2   Invite each child to make up their favourite pudding by, in turn, choosing three of the pictures.

3 Encourage some of the children to share with the group what they have chosen and why.

TIP
You could play the game with the last person to sit down each time being out of the game and their chair removed from the circle. The game then ends when there is only one player left.

THEME

Explain that in this session they will be thinking about why it is important to look after themselves and that what they eat can have an effect on their body and also how they feel.

Healthy eating, healthy mind

You will need: cooking ingredients and equipment

Invite a leader who is confident at cooking to bring in some ingredients and teach the group how to make something that is healthy, eg a fruit salad or a smoothie.

While the group are making their healthy food, use the following questions to help the group to realise how what we eat can influence how we feel:

- Why do you think it is important to eat lots of fruit and vegetables?

- Do you think food can influence your mood and, if so, why?

- What do you think it means to eat a balanced diet?

- In what ways do you think having a healthy diet is good for your mind?

- Why do you think breakfast is the most important meal of the day?

For some interesting facts to share with the children about how food affects our mood, visit https://www.mind.org.uk/information-support/tips-for-everyday-living/food-and-mood/about-food-and-mood/

TIP
Ask the group to make up some of their own exercises to add to the active challenge.

REFLECTION

Active challenge

If you have a really sporty or active group, lead them in this active challenge:

- do ten star jumps
- run on the spot for 20 seconds
- sit cross-legged on the floor and try to stand up without using your hands
- do five press-ups.

After the challenge, discuss the following questions together:

- Did you find that challenging?
- Do you feel tired or do you have more energy?
- Do you think it matters how you look after yourself? Why?

Habit cards

You will need: felt-tip pens, pencils, thin card, stickers

Invite the group to make some healthy reminder habit cards that they can take home. They could use the following sentences, or you could challenge your group to think of their own.

- Today I choose to move more by doing the following...
- Today I choose to be kind by doing the following...
- Today I choose to smile at...
- Today I choose to eat the following healthy foods...

Challenge

You will need: felt-tip pens, pencils

Encourage the children to take a healthy challenge for a week. Help them to make a chart showing the days of the week and the following challenges:

- eat more vegetables
- be more active
- be kind
- spend 10 minutes being quiet each day
- try a new fruit
- say something encouraging to a friend
- try a new sport or activity
- eat fewer sweets and less chocolate
- drink three glasses of water a day

Suggest they mark on their chart whenever they have done one of the challenges; invite anyone who wants to to share their completed chart next time you meet.

DIG DEEPER

Remind the group that Jesus was also human like them, and ask for suggestions of the sorts of things he would have done (he ate, drank, had friends, had emotions – would have gone to the toilet).
Discuss the following questions together:

• Do you think Jesus looked after himself?

• Do you think God wants us to look after ourselves? Why?

FURTHER IDEAS

Future weeks
You could spend several weeks exploring cookery and baking, or exploring different sports and fun aerobics (there are several fitness workouts available online, but make sure they are suitable for the age and ability of the children in your group).

ROOTED JUNIOR JOURNAL

If you are using the **Rooted Junior Journal** with your group, you could include some time in your session for the children to work through pages 41 to 48, which include a recipe for pizza. Alternatively, you could encourage the children to work through these pages at home, between sessions, if they would like to.

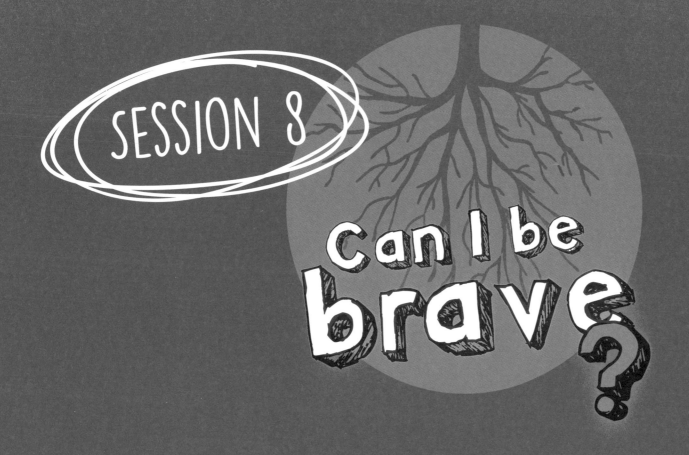

SESSION 8

Can I be brave?

OBJECTIVES

For the children to learn a new skill, to step out of their comfort zone and learn how to be brave.

Begin your session with one of the following activities or games:

Bushtucker trial

You will need: a blindfold, plastic tubs, a selection of different textured materials or foods

1 In advance, fill several plastic tubs with a series of different materials such as baked beans, play dough, feathers, water, slime or other materials. Do make sure you check for allergies before you start.

2 Ask for a volunteer and blindfold them.

3 Challenge them to guess what is in each tub, using only their hands.

Chocolate relay

You will need: small chocolate sweets, drinking straws, bowls

1 Organise your group into teams of an equal number.

2 For each team, place a bowl full of sweets in front of them and an empty bowl at a distance.

3 Give each team member a straw.

4 Challenge team members to take it in turns to make a sweet stick to the bottom of their straw (by sucking – ensuring that the sweets are too big to go up the straws!) and transport it to the other bowl.

5 Set a time limit; the winning team is the one with the most sweets in the second bowl.

THEME

TIP
If you don't have a leader with a particular skill, invite someone from your local community to teach one such as circus skills, music making, drama, craft, sport.

Explain that they are going to be thinking about being brave by trying out new experiences and learning new skills. Reassure the children that trying something new can feel scary, but by being bold and brave they can grow and learn by their successes and their failures!

Invite a leader who is confident in a particular and appropriate skill, such as juggling, skateboarding, street dance, drawing, painting, playing an instrument, story writing etc, to run a workshop to teach the children some new skills. Alternatively, run a new skills workshop and invite several people offering a variety of skills to share and teach them to the children. During the workshop give the children the opportunity to ask the following questions:

- What was it like when you were first learning how to...?

- Were you scared when you first started?

- How long did it take you to become as good as you are now?

REFLECTION

Top five challenges

You will need: paper, pencils, coloured pens

Encourage the group to think about five new skills they would like to learn, and invite them to make a poster or list of these.

As they work, explain that being brave can open the door to lots of new things and experiences, and when we try something new for the first time it often isn't as scary as we first thought.

Then as a whole group discuss the following questions together:

- What did it feel like when you tried something new for the first time?

- What's the scariest thing you have ever done?

- When have you had to be brave?

- Have you ever helped someone else when they have had to choose to be brave?

DIG DEEPER

As the group make their posters, discuss the following questions together:

- Do you think God answers prayers?

- Do you have a situation that you could share with the group about when God answered your prayer?

- Can you remember a time when you prayed about something you were scared about? What happened?

TIP
Share the story of Peter walking on the water to Jesus from Matthew 14:22–33.

TIP
You could print out some Bible verses that the children could take home to remind them that God can help them be brave.

- Is there something happening in your life that you would like to ask God for bravery for?

Ask one of the leaders to give an example from their own life where they have been brave and trusted God.

FURTHER IDEAS

A talent show
Encourage the children to practise and rehearse for a talent show on an agreed date.

Bible characters
Introduce other characters from the Bible who have been brave – Esther, Joseph, David

Adventure
Visit a climbing or a trampoline facility.

ROOTED JUNIOR JOURNAL

If you are using the *Rooted Junior Journal* with your group, you could include some time in your session for the children to work through pages 49 to 54. Alternatively, you could encourage the children to work through these pages at home, between sessions, if they would like to.

SESSION 9

What does the future hold?

OBJECTIVES

For the children to think about the future, build their confidence and dream big!

ICEBREAKER

Mini Olympics

You will need: plastic/paper cups, sticky tape, playing cards, a hula hoop

Set up some games for the children to choose from:

- **Towers** – encourage the children individually to build the highest tower they can using paper straws and sticky tape or playing cards.
- **Flip cup** – invite the children to flip as many cups as possible so that they land face down.
- **Hoop-a-cup** – set up a series of plastic cups on the floor and mark a throwing line on the floor. Invite the children, one at a time, to throw the hoop over the cups from the throwing line. The most cups hooped wins.

Careers

Play a game of charades, asking the children to act out a job or career they would like to have in the future, for the rest of the group to guess.

When the job or career has been guessed correctly, ask them to tell the rest of the group why they would like to do that job or career when they are older.

THEME

Explain that in this session they are going to be looking at hopes and dreams. Encourage the group that their hopes and dreams don't just have to be things that are in the distant future; they can be things they would like to achieve by the end of today, next week or next year! Remind them that dreams can need effort to achieve!

Dreams can come true

You will need: paper, pencils, coloured pens

Using one large sheet of paper for the whole group or an individual sheet of paper for each child, encourage the children to write down their dreams and hopes for the future, to create a poster. Challenge them to think big and small, and to really use their imaginations; leaders can join in too!

As the children are working, discuss the following questions together (you may need to adjust the wording for children who are not in traditional schooling structures):

- What might life look like after you leave primary school?
- Is there anything you will miss about primary school?
- Is there anything you would like to achieve before you start secondary school?
- Is there anything you are looking forward to about going to secondary school?

Ask me anything

Invite a secondary school student to visit the group, so that the children can quiz them about what life is like at secondary school. Here are a few question ideas to get the children started:

- What is secondary school like?
- Do you get lots of homework?
- Have you ever got lost?
- Did you find it difficult to make new friends?
- Who should I talk to if I am feeling worried at school?

Alternatively, invite someone you know who has a really interesting job that you think may appeal to the children. Give them the opportunity to share what their job is like and for the children to ask questions.

Here are a few question ideas to get the children started:

- When you were at school, what did you want to do for a job?
- Did you have to go to college or university to study for the job you do now?
- Have you always done the same job since you left education?
- What is the best bit about your job?
- If you could choose a second job or career, what would it be and why?

TIP
Ask the children to give you some ideas of jobs or careers they would like to do in the future. This will give you an idea of who to invite to share their work experiences with the group.

REFLECTION

Tell a story using one of the following film characters, or any other heroes you can think of: Woody from *Toy Story*; Nemo from *Finding Nemo*; Dory from *Finding Dory*; Merida from *Brave*. Explain how the character overcame challenges through determination to achieve their dreams, and how the children can do that, too!

Discuss the following questions together:

- Do you think it's important to have dreams?
- What lessons can you learn from the characters you have heard about?
- What does it feel like when you achieve something that you didn't think was possible?

TIP
Share this fact with the group: Did you know that God cares about every detail of your life? the Bible tells us he even knows how many hairs are on your head (Luke 12:7)!

DIG DEEPER

Discuss the following questions together:

- Have you ever told God about your hopes and dreams?
- Do you think God cares about your hopes and dreams?

FURTHER IDEAS

Plan, dream, achieve
Encourage the children to think of something they were planning to throw away. Challenge them to think of a way of turning it into something useful, and to make a plan for doing that. This activity helps them to think about how they can plan, dream and try to achieve their goal.

ROOTED JUNIOR JOURNAL

If you are using the *Rooted Junior Journal* with your group, you could include some time in your session for the children to work through pages 55 to 60. Alternatively, you could encourage the children to work through these pages at home, between sessions, if they would like to.

Where now?

OBJECTIVES

For the children to celebrate all they have discovered about themselves and each other through Rooted Junior.

This session runs slightly differently from the other sessions. Pick and choose from the following ideas to give the children an opportunity to reflect and celebrate, and to plan what's next!!

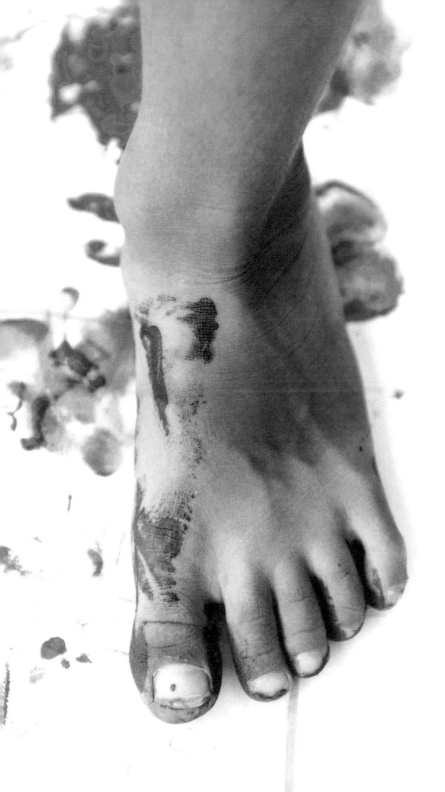

Gingerbread decoration

Put everyone's name into a hat. Invite each child to pick out a name and decorate a gingerbread figure to represent that person. During this activity encourage the children to share with the rest of the group their person's good qualities.

Pass the Parcel

Create a parcel that has a reflective question in each layer about their time in the Rooted Junior sessions. Include things like: What have you enjoyed the most? What have you learned about yourself that you didn't know before?

Pass the Parcel with challenges – include with each layer a challenge or forfeit, eg do five burpees, run on the spot for 10 seconds.

Pin the heart

Stick a large outline of a person on the wall. Challenge your group, in turn and blindfolded, to stick a heart shape on to the body to reflect areas they have looked at during Rooted Junior. After they have taken their blindfold off, encourage them to share with the rest of the group one thing they have learned about themselves since they started at Rooted Junior.

Picture frames

Source and print some images that reflect the different things that have happened during your Rooted Junior sessions. Give each child a blank picture frame (or help them to make their own), then invite them to choose an image for their frame. Encourage them to explain why that image reflects their time in the Rooted Junior sessions.

Remind them that there is no right or wrong answer – it's about how they have felt during their time, and everyone's answer will be different.

Photobooks

Create photobooks, similar to school yearbooks, with spaces for the children to write messages to each other. Include space for them to write memories of things that have happened during their time together.

Mirrors

Give each child a mirror (or mirror card or reflective plastic) and a larger sheet of card. Encourage the group to stick the mirror on to the card, and to write around the outside of the mirror something positive they have learned about themselves. Challenge them to put their mirror up at home and to read their positive thing every day. Explain that this will help them to feel more confident about who they are and how God sees them.

Posters

Challenge the children to design posters to advertise Rooted Junior, to help others to understand more about it.

Prayer boxes

Help the children to create and decorate individual prayer boxes, to keep and take home. Encourage them to add a prayer every day, and maybe once a month to read through their prayers to see

if God has answered any or all of them. Remind them that prayers don't have to be about themselves – they can and should pray for others, too.

Cairns

Invite the children to paint or decorate a stone or pebble with a memory from their time at Rooted Junior. Explain how in the Old Testament a cairn (or a pile of rocks) would have been used as a reminder of when God had taught the people something, and would have helped to teach future generations of their journey and experience. Encourage the children to take their stones or pebbles home.

Time to talk

During this session it is important to get a feel for where your group is at in terms of moving forward together both in their faith and as a community.

Here are some extra questions you could use to help you with that:

- If you could ask God any question, what would it be?
- Has your attitude towards the way you think about God changed?
- Is there anything you have learned about yourself during our sessions?
- What kinds to things would you like to do next in Rooted Junior?

TIP
Share some Bible verses with the group to help them remember that God is with them wherever they go! Psalm 119:105 and Psalm 139:1–5.

- Is there anything you would like to know more of about God?
- Do you feel more confident about yourself since you started coming to the Rooted Junior sessions?
- Which session did you enjoy most, and why?
- Would you recommend Rooted Junior to a friend?
- Describe Rooted Junior in three words.
- Do you think you are now able to make some healthy choices about the food you eat and how you look after yourself?
- Do you know what to do if you are worried or anxious about anything?
- Do you know how to describe to someone how you are feeling?

Make time to explore with your group ideas and suggestions for planning what happens next. Are there any topics or themes they would like to continue exploring? It's important for the children to feel as though they are taking ownership of this group and are integral in shaping and forming what their Rooted Junior group looks like going forward. Remember, this is not the end, it's just the beginning!

Rooted Junior Hub Cards – Revisited

Remember that the **Rooted Junior Hub Cards** can be used in all and any of the Rooted Junior sessions. For this session you could revisit the faith-based questions you asked in Session 1 and see whether or not their answers are still the same. If they have changed, encourage them to tell you why.

Faith journeys

Invite one of the leaders to share their faith journey with the group.

ROOTED JUNIOR JOURNAL

If you are using the **Rooted Junior Journal** with your group, you could include some time in your session for the children to work through pages 61 to 64. Alternatively, you could encourage the children to work through these pages at home, between sessions, if they would like to.

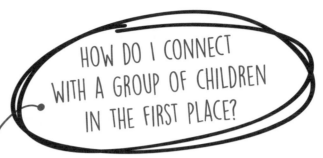

Unless you're already working with an established group of children, you might be wondering how you can begin working with children in your local community.

Developing a Rooted Junior Hub

To help make initial connections, we recommend that you create a Rooted Junior Hub, which is a safe space for children to gather. This might take the form of a children's club, or lunchtime or after-school club.

This could be a connection space, perhaps from a school where you do assemblies or as a follow-up to a pop-up mission, or similar. It should be made clear from the start that this is a Christian-run club.

A Rooted Junior Hub should:

- provide a safe, welcoming, accessible environment for children to gather

- provide age-appropriate activities for children to engage in that are also appropriate for their context

- use contemporary media and interests to help facilitate honest and authentic conversations

- offer children a chance to go deeper by joining a Rooted Junior group.

What kind of space should be used for a Rooted Junior Hub?

Any space – indoor or outdoor – that can be made safe, welcoming and accessible for children!

Ideally, your location should be somewhere that the children in your community are already familiar with, feel comfortable coming to and are able to be dropped off and picked up at by their parent or guardian easily. An example might be a drop-in club in primary school or in a local community space.

Consider what facilities you will need based on what kinds of activities you want to offer.

What kinds of activities should a Rooted Junior Hub provide?

Children aged 8 to 11 benefit from a loose framework of activities. They thrive better with some structure and having the reassurance of knowing how the session will run. A suggested outline for your Hub sessions is:

- welcome and chat
- game or activity
- snack
- talk/chat around Hub cards
- reflection time/craft/game.

A Rooted Junior Hub should be based around activities that connect with the children in your community. For example, if there is a group of children who are interested in board games, your Hub could provide activities around this theme.

Whatever your theme, you should try to find at least one volunteer who is skilled in that particular area and is able to share their talents with the children.

Ideas for Hub themes include:

- board games
- a particular sport or street dance
- cooking
- creating videos/media
- music
- wildlife/nature
- construction or Minecraft.

How do Rooted Junior Hub activities help to facilitate honest and authentic conversations?

Meeting children where they are and journeying alongside them is one of the core principles of Rooted Junior.

Engaging with children through activities they are already interested in and care about leads to authentic and meaningful conversation and relationships.

The key is to invite children to share their interests with you, asking insightful, thoughtful and open questions and giving them time and space to listen to what they say.

Each session could start with a check-in activity, when the children have the opportunity to share with the group what they have been up to or how they are feeling. You could use the *Rooted Junior Hub Cards* or create your own emoji cards based

on emotions. This kind of activity can help the children to feel heard and valued.

If your Rooted Junior Hub is, for example, based around a particular sport, and you decide to ask the children to share who some of their favourite players are, your questions might include:

- Why do you like this particular player?
- What is it that makes them stand out in their sport?
- How does it make you feel watching this sportsperson compete?
- What kind of person does this player make you want to be?
- Do you know any interesting facts about this sportsperson?

Obviously, you will need to carefully consider which questions to ask, based on your Hub theme and context.

If you'd like a few pointers for how to open up this kind of conversation, you can buy a set of *Rooted Junior Hub Cards* (which work with any theme) from the Scripture Union website.

A note on safeguarding and insurance...

All Rooted Junior Hubs must abide by the safeguarding policy of your organisation, and you must have the express permission of the child's parent or guardian for them to attend.

Depending on your activities and location, you may need specific insurance cover (outside of that which your organisation normally provides). Consult with your insurance provider for more information.